UPSIDE DOWN

UPSIDE DOWN

WHY NEW HOMEBUYERS WILL END UP WITH NEGATIVE EQUITY

Randall J Stein

© 2017 Randall J Stein
All rights reserved.

ISBN: 1977841538
ISBN 13: 9781977841537

This book is dedicated to potential new home buyers whose capacity for self-delusion is commensurate with their agents. The goal is to give home buyers the ammunition needed to help them avoid overpaying for a home through the understanding of economic cycles and to encourage the encompassment of patience.

"Home-Price Destruction"

It is agonizingly obvious that the indicators that gave us a clue into the economic collapse of 2007–2008 are once again providing us with a bird's-eye view to another impending disaster, namely

- housing prices are at ridiculous levels;
- credit-card debt is at a record high;
- stock and bond markets are at record levels;
- gold has rallied to new highs;
- a huge number of student loans are defaulting;

- world politics are increasingly unstable (e.g., a nuclear North Korea);
- terrorism is occurring throughout the world;
- federal unfunded liabilities for future taxpayers are unsustainable; and
- federal unfunded liabilities are estimated at $127 trillion—approximately $1.1 million per taxpayer (usdebtclock.org).

With home prices steadily increasing over time, people are deluded into thinking that property inflation will go on indefinitely, becoming the less risky place to put their savings. However, we are now in the second-biggest housing boom of all time, and prices cannot stay at this level. It is well known that home costs should not exceed more than 43 percent of income, and rising interest rates on the horizon means cheap money will soon be a thing of the past. This environment has allowed foreign buyers with loads of "funny money" to buy up property at a level where US buyers cannot compete.

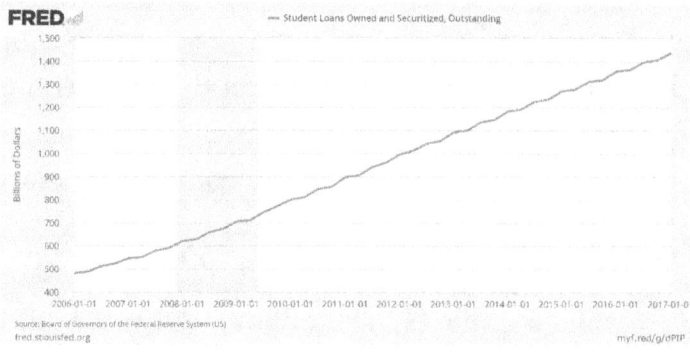

Rents are now rising to unaffordable levels, and home equity is used like an ATM whereby mortgages are refinanced often as prices rise and rates fall. Seminars and television shows on flipping homes have proliferated and are a key indicator of a speculative top. And since it's now so easy to buy homes without cash, flippers buy homes and never bother to fix them up, using exotic financing and selling them without making a payment. In many large cities, flippers make up 8 percent of the market.

Home prices are way above what the fundamentals can justify. The true value of a single-family home should be whatever the price results from the average homeowner in a market putting down

20 percent and taking out no more mortgage debt than would result in a maximum debt-to-income ratio of 43 percent. Under the qualified-mortgage rule, most mortgages have a maximum backend DTI ratio of 43 percent.[1]

Let's give an example of the Bay area where the average home is $1.5 million, and you would have to earn $294,600. With the typical homeowner's insurance costs and credit-card debts, the average person can afford a $778,000 home, almost 50 percent below the average home price in the Bay area.

A modest home near San Jose just sold for $2.5 million, nearly $800,000 over the asking price.[2] This happened due to the home being just three miles from Apple's new spaceship campus. Incomes aren't rising to the level of home prices. In fact, they're not even close.

The government debt to gross domestic product (GDP) is at levels not seen in over thirty years.

UPSIDE DOWN

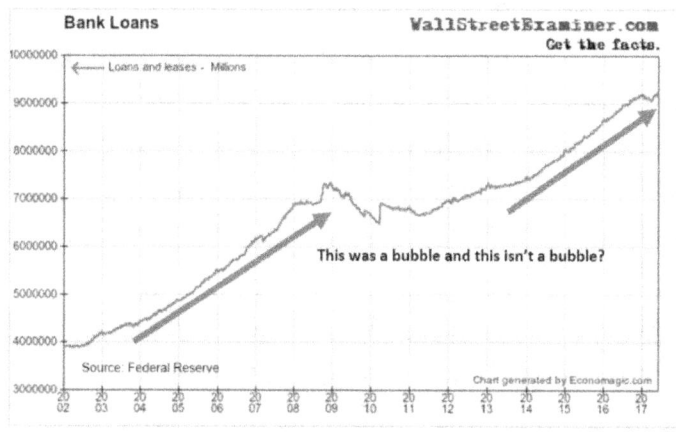

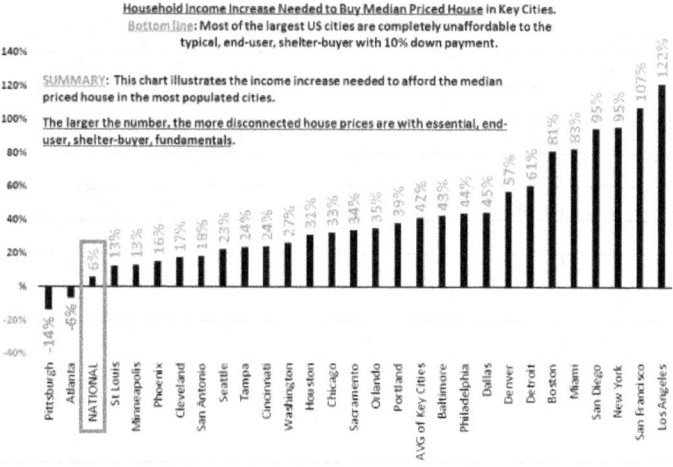

The $90 billion over hang of maturing commercial mortgages will expose the inherent weakness in the US real-estate market, the result of long-term cheap money. This time, the property-asset bubble is truly global and affects all investment classes of real estate driven by investors (China) using low-cost funds and are also awash with money. Remember, housing bubbles take about five to six years to reach a peak and generally overshoot the downside when they implode.

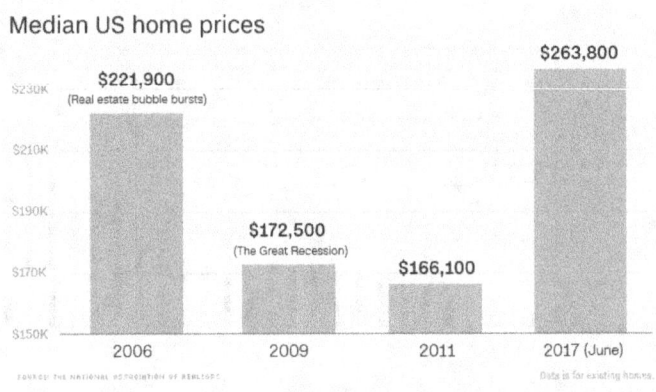

Barry Sternlich, CEO of the Starwood Property Trust, which finances real-estate development, calls Manhattan's luxury condo situation "a catastrophe" that "will get worse."[3]

UPSIDE DOWN

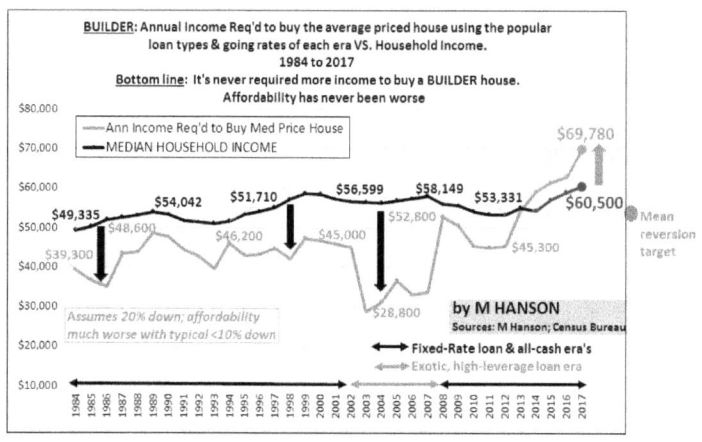

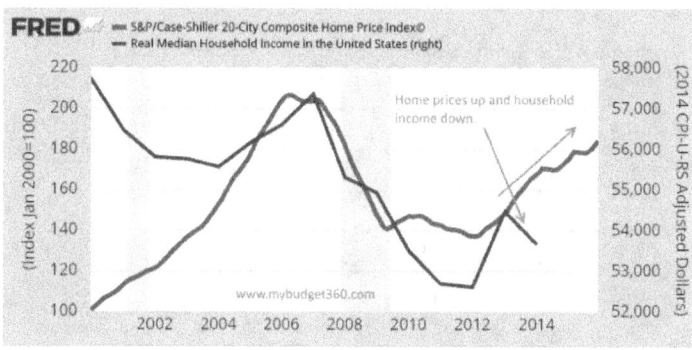

In *The Facts about Speculation*, Thomas Gibson writes, "The most glaringly apparent cause of loss revealed by the investigation of these accounts was the almost universal habit of making purchases at high prices after a material rise has already occurred."[4]

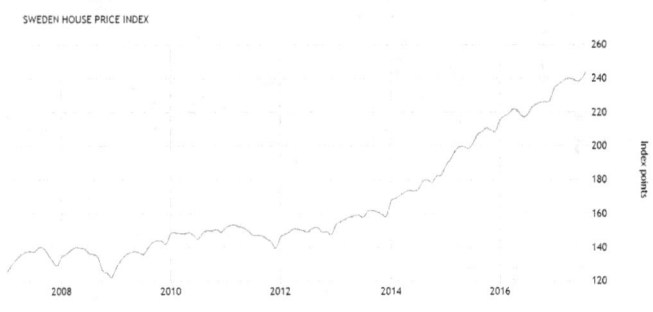

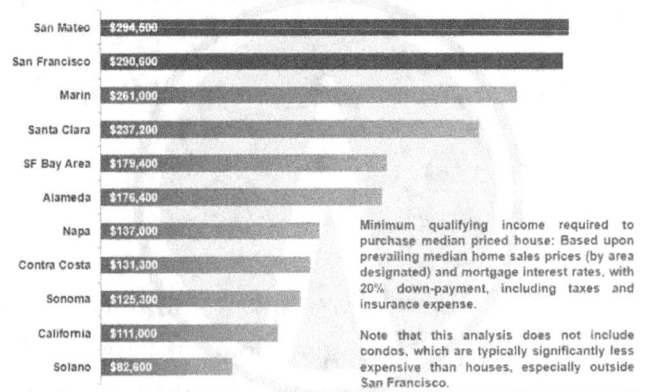

UPSIDE DOWN

China Shadow Banking Credit Gap Could Trigger the Bust

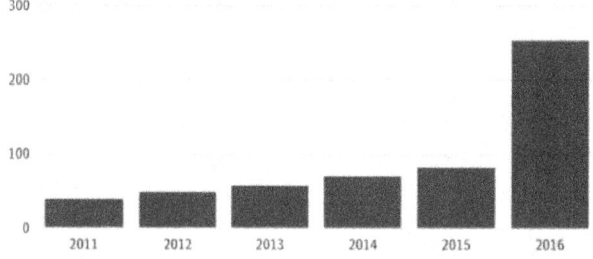

Source: The Daily Telegraph, July 17, 2017

Dallas - Case-Shiller Home Price Index
Not seasonally adjusted; released May 30, 2017

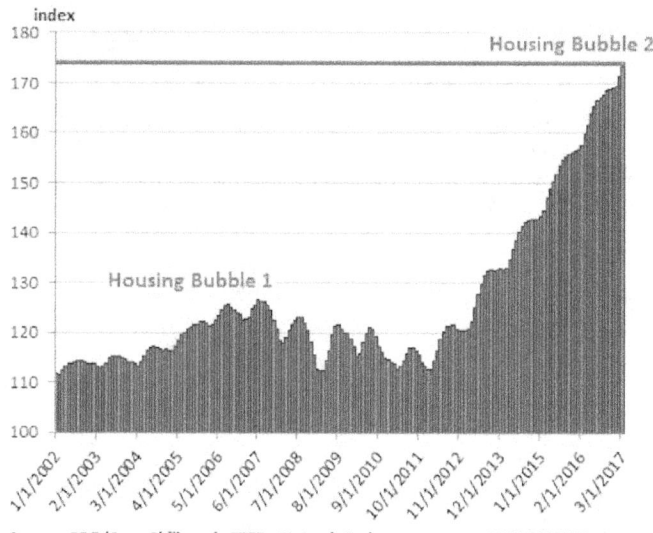

Source: S&P/Case-Shiller, via FRED, St. Louis Fed   WOLFSTREET.com

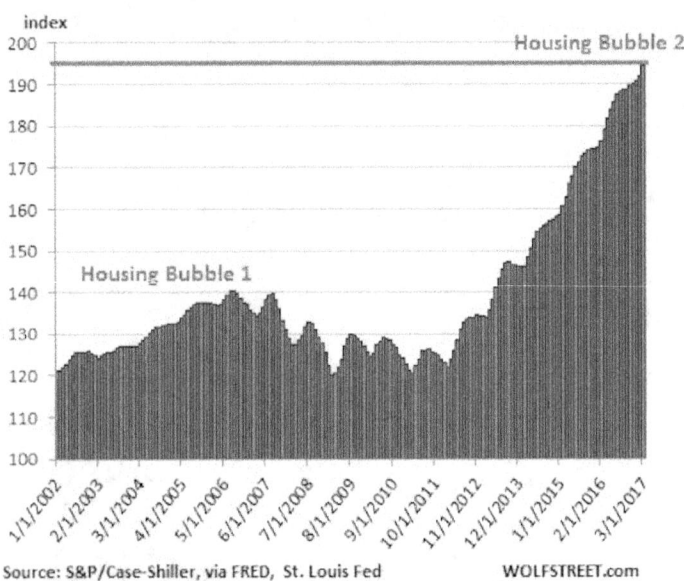

UPSIDE DOWN

New York Condos - Case-Shiller Home Price Index
Not seasonally adjusted; released May 30, 2017

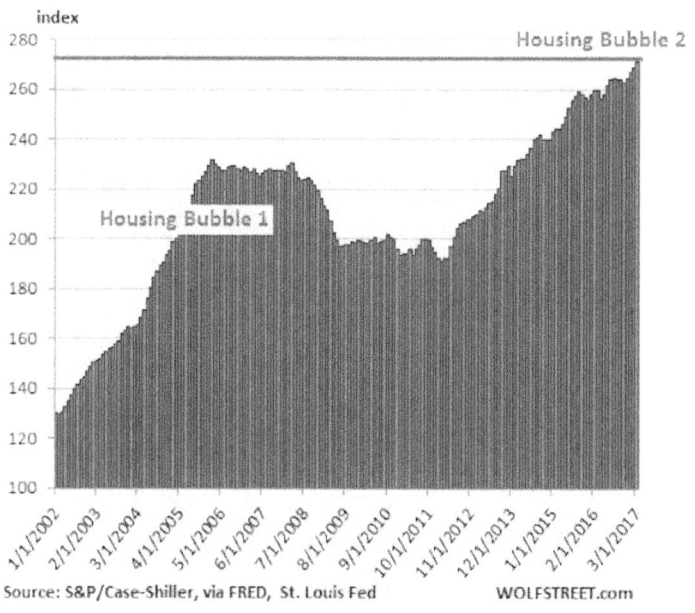

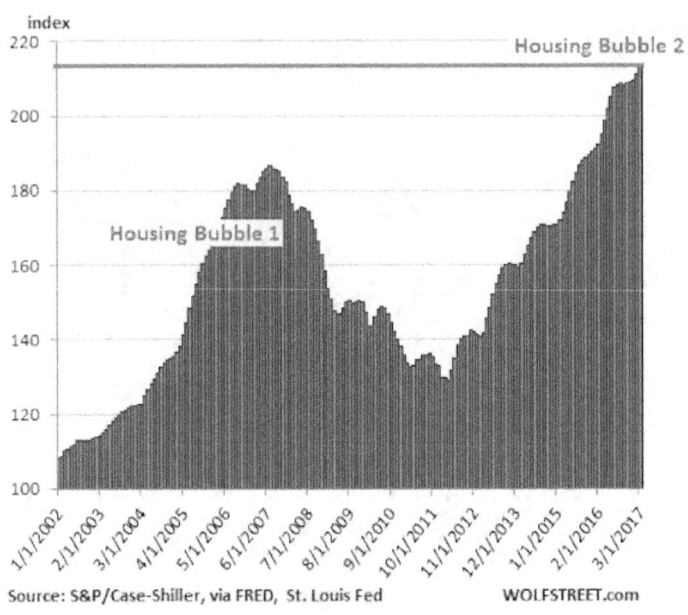

UPSIDE DOWN

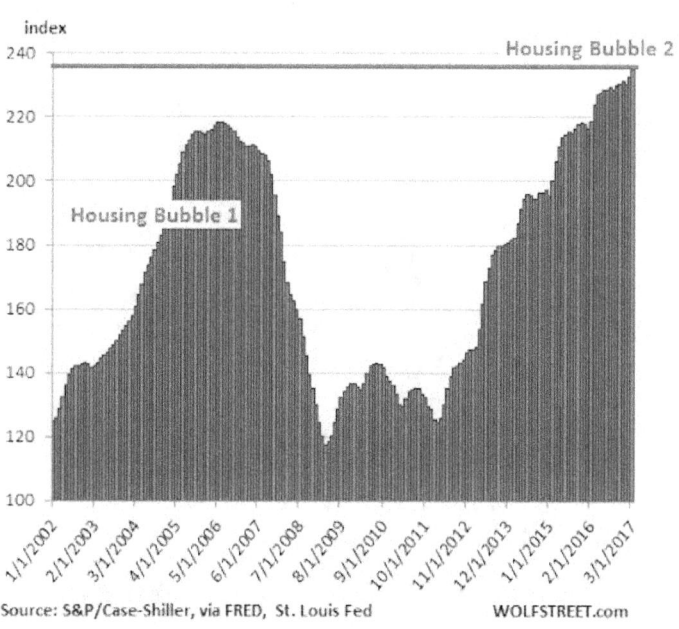

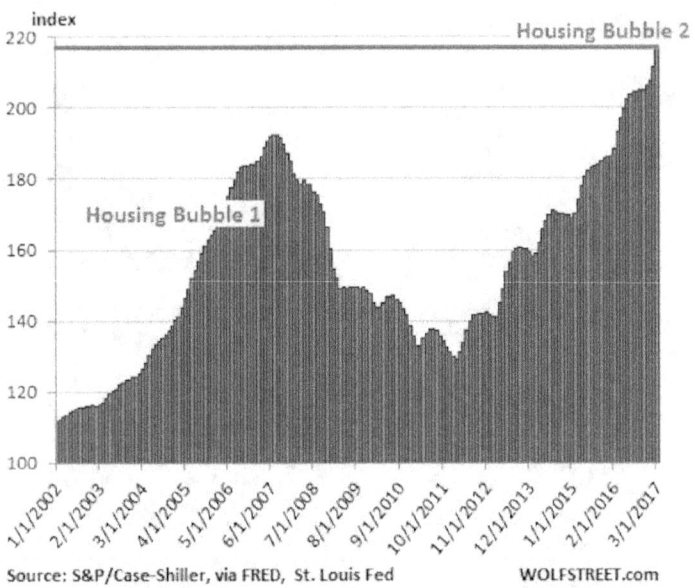

Subprime Auto Market

Subprime auto-loan default rates match those seen just before the 2007–2009 recession. Recently the ninety-day auto-loan delinquency rates eclipsed 3.8 percent,[5] their highest levels since the financial crisis, putting auto-loan investors and shareholders of subprime auto lenders at risk. According to data from Experian, the balance of deep subprime loans—those given to people with credit scores of 300 to 500—increased 14.6 percent from 2015 to 2016.[6]

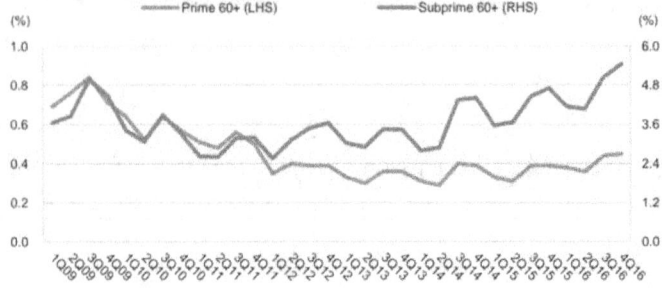

Morgan Stanley said about the following in a March report:

> Across prime and subprime ABS, [60-plus-day] delinquencies are currently printing at 0.54 and 4.51 percent, respectively, with the latter approaching crisis-era peak levels (4.69 percent). Default rates are also picking up in similar fashion (prime: 1.52 percent; subprime: 11.96 percent), printing close to crisis levels.

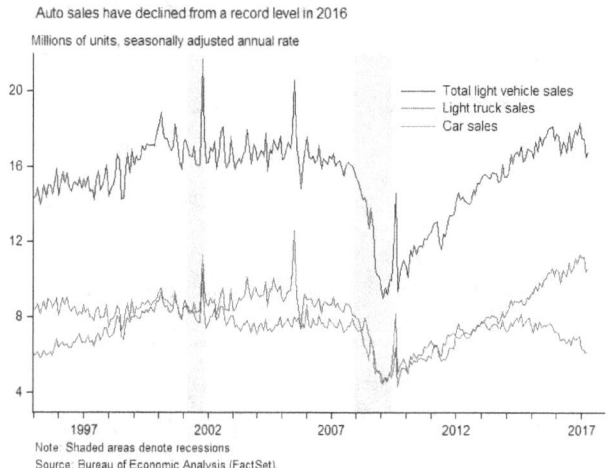

While prime severities slowly crept past 50 percent recently, subprime severities have breached 60 percent, a level we haven't seen since late 2009. With both default rates and loss severities trending up, it is no surprise to see annualized net loss rates moving in the same direction.[7]

Subprime lenders are willing to take a chance on these risky borrowers because, once they default, the lenders can repossess their cars and persuade judges in forty-six states to give them the power to seize borrowers' paychecks to cover the balance of the car loan.

The top bank holding derivatives is Citigroup, the same financial institution that got into huge trouble with toxic derivatives and subprime debt. And it now has over $47 trillion in holdings.[8] This means that Citigroup and other huge banking enterprises are holding massive amounts of this speculative money, and the US government is backing it all. (The top twenty-five US banks have $222 trillion of exposure to derivatives.)

Wall Street has rewarded lax lending standards that let people get loans without anyone verifying incomes or job histories. For instance, Santander Bank recently vetted incomes on less than one out of every ten loans packaged into $1 billion of bonds, according to Moody's Investors Service. The largest portion was for Chrysler vehicles.

State authorities also said an internal Santander review in 2013 found that ten out of eleven loan applications from a Massachusetts dealer contained inflated or unverifiable incomes.

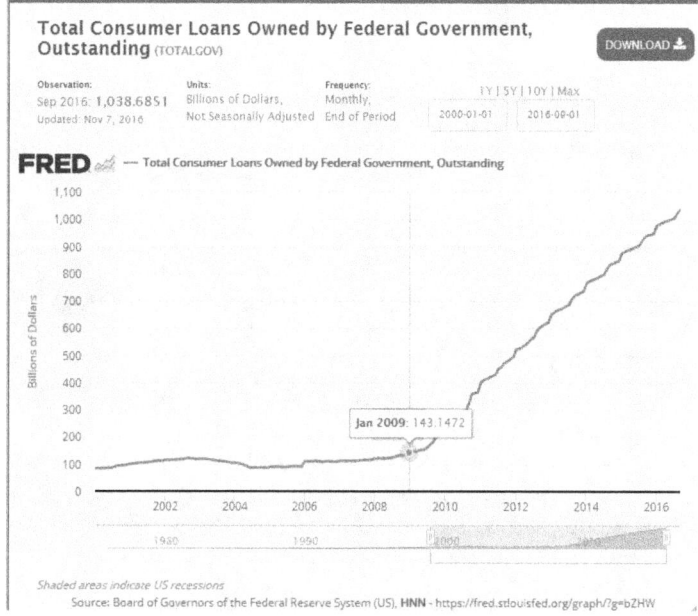

The Liberty Street Economics post said:

Sixty-plus-day delinquencies for subprime auto loans is at its highest level in at least seven years.
"The data suggest some notable deterioration in the performance of subprime auto loans. This translates into a large number

of households, with roughly six million individuals at least ninety days late on their auto loan payments."

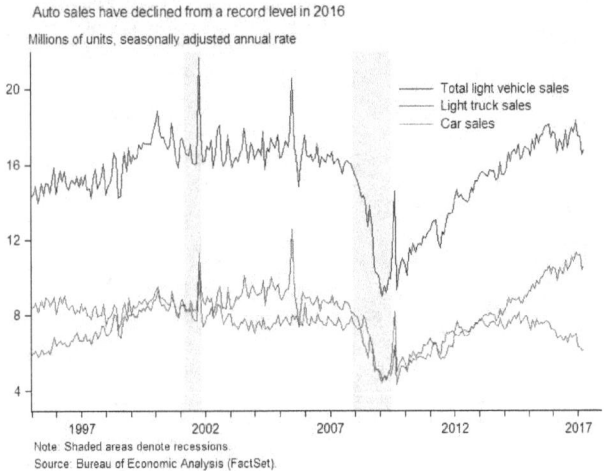

www.businessinsider.com/subprime-auto-loans-are-a-reminder-of-the-housing-crisis-...Apr 15, 2017

Stocks

Robert Shiller, a Yale finance professor, stated, "The market is way overpriced, the S&P 500 now trades at a cyclically adjusted price to earnings ratio of 30 compared to a historic fair value of this measure of about 16."[9]

David Stockman pounds the table:

> The S&P 500s ratio of EBIDTA to TEV (market equity plus net debt) is now truly in the sky-box section of history. It has never been close to the current level of 11.3X—except during a few months of sheer stock market mania at the turn of the century. Yet fools

claim to see not even a hint of bubbles anywhere on the horizon.[10]

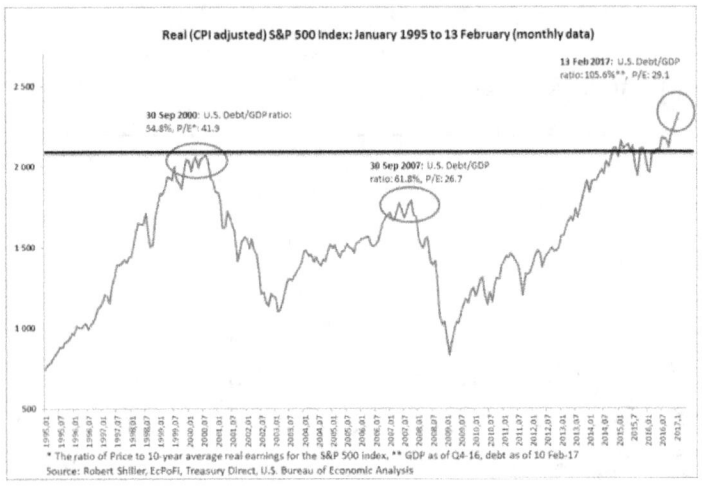

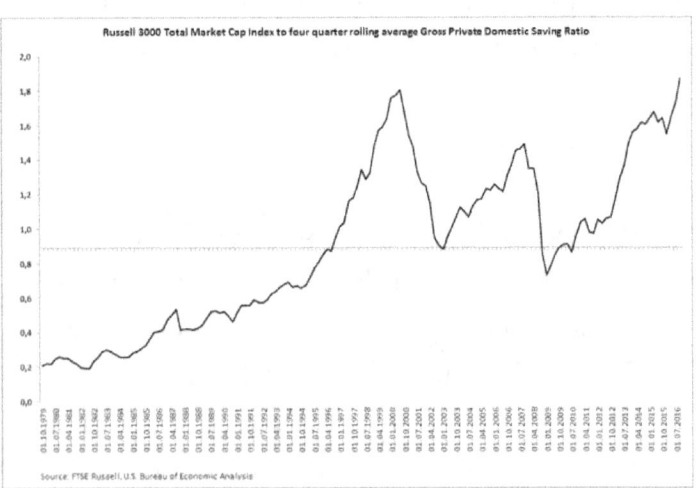

The stock markets are at nosebleed levels while productivity is failing to keep up. Goldman Sachs warned that the stock market has an "elevated valuation on almost every metric."[11] A report written by a team led by chief equity strategist David Kostin stated, "The forward P/E multiple of the S&P 500 has risen by 80% since 2011 (to 18X) and now trades at the 89th percentile compared with the past 40 years while the typical stock is at the 99th percentile of historic valuation."[12]

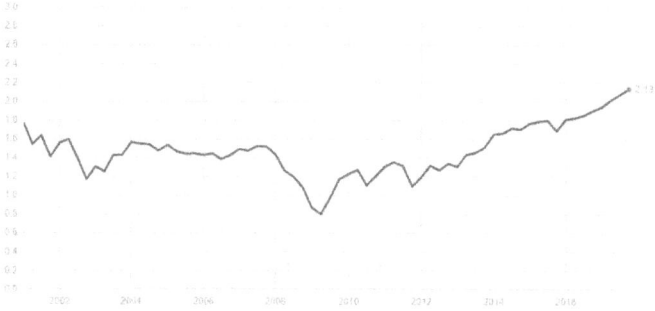

FactSet noted that the twelve-month price-earning (P/E) ratio for the market is 22.1, well above the ten-year average of 16.7.[13] John Hussman, chairman of the Hussman Funds, asserted, "Presently, we observe the broadest market valuation extreme in history with the steepest median valuations on record, and the most reliable capitalization-weighted measures within a few percent of their 2000 peaks."

On top of such warnings as "extreme valuations, bullish sentiment, and consumer confidence," Hussman adds, "Market action has deteriorated in interest sensitive sectors...more than one third of stocks are already below their 200 day moving averages."[14]

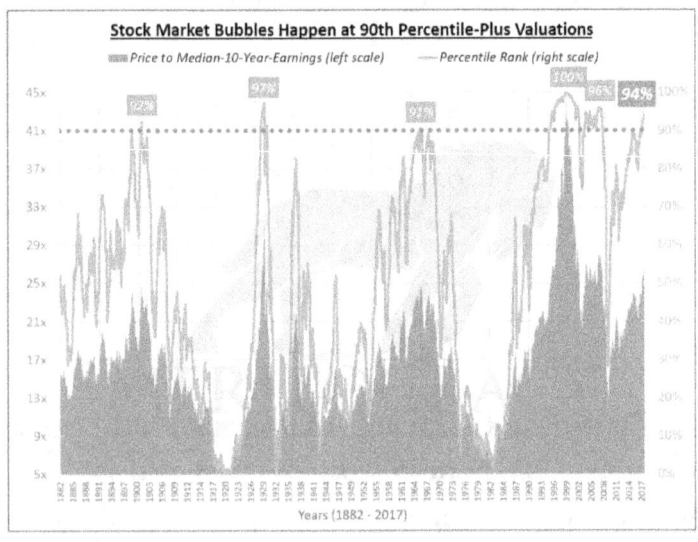

According to the World Bank, the total US stock market is now valued at more than 150

percent of annual gross domestic product.[15] That is way above historic norms and about the same as it was at the market extreme of 2000.

According to StarCapital Research, the United States has the least affordable equity market in the world, coming in least among the forty countries and regions it analyzed. For the United States, the most vital warning sign could be the cyclically adjusted price-to-earnings ratio, or CAPE, which compares stock prices to corporate earnings over the past ten years. Based on this, the United States comes in at 28.0, cheaper than only Denmark (36.1) and Ireland (34.5). Ratios at this level portend steep market declines.[16]

When looking at price-to-book ratios, the United States is the second-most expensive country in the world with a reading of 3.1. Indonesia tops the United States with a ratio of 3.3.[17] The stock market has no competition because of low interest rates.

The Shiller price-to-earnings ratio has been this high only during the dot-com bubble of 2000 and the 1929 market crash. These signals indicate a top is coming soon and you should be moving to cash to take advantage of these markets once they collapse, and then you can buy on the cheap.

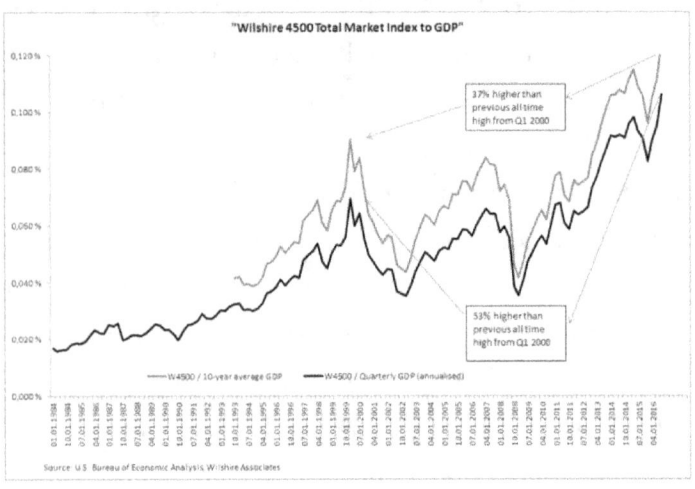

Driving the narrative of a stock market inflating at an unsustainable pace is the fact stock prices keep going up, even though the S&P 500 stock index is trading at more than twenty-one times its earnings over the past four quarters—or 28 percent higher than its average P-E of 16.6 since 1965, says Oppenheimer, a Wall Street firm.

China's Housing Market along with Our Bond Market are about to Crack!

"Equity markets are priced for too much hope, high-yield bond markets for too much growth, and all asset prices elevated to artificial levels that only a model-driven, historically biased investor would believe could lead to returns resembling the past six years," said Bill Gross, manager of the Janus Global Unconstrained Bond Fund.[18]

China's ongoing debt is nearly 300 percent of GDP,[19] and the credit bubble is about to burst. Also the property boom has evidently topped out across seventy cities and M1 money-supply growth is turning down, indicating storm clouds are on the horizon.

Ambrose Evans Pritchard has stated, "The world has never been so leveraged to dollar borrowing costs. The Bank of International Settlements show that debt ratios in both rich countries and emerging markets are roughly 35 percentage points of GDP higher than they were at the onset of the Lehman crisis."[20]

The Federal Reserve has been raising short-term interest rates since December, and the bond market hasn't seemed to notice. About 60 percent of fund managers surveyed earlier this year by Bank of America Corporation researchers said they thought investment-grade and high-yield corporate bonds were overvalued.[21] US investment-grade bond funds received an unprecedented $163.8 billion of flows this year.

"The real risk that China poses to the U.S. and global economies is that its rapid economic growth since the 2008-2009 global economic recession has been powered by a credit bubble of epic proportions," wrote Desmond Lachman, an American Enterprise Institute fellow who previously served as a deputy director of the IMF.22

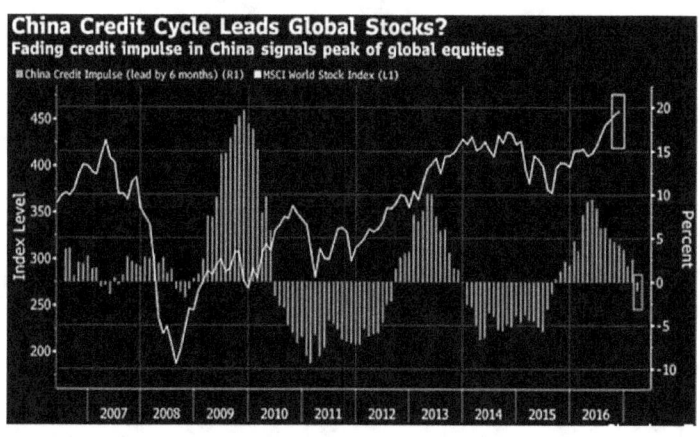

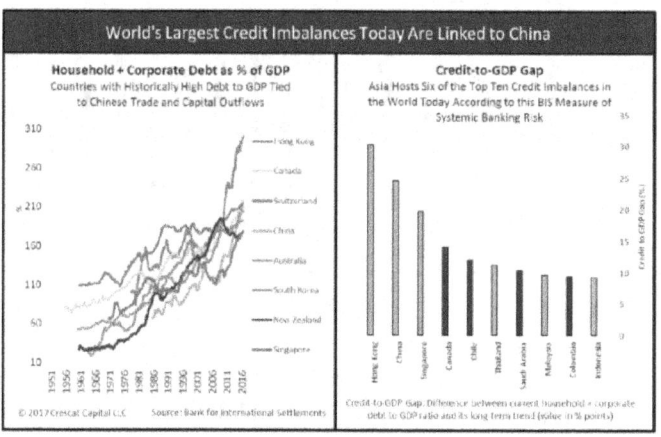

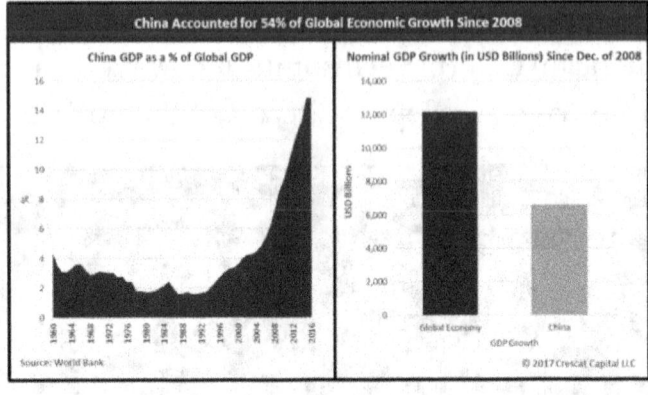

What does "epic" mean? By one account, China has expanded credit by nearly 100 percent of the nation's GDP since the end of the credit crisis.

Since 2007, China has added $24 trillion in debt at all levels, which is more than the US government's *total debt* of just under $20 trillion.23

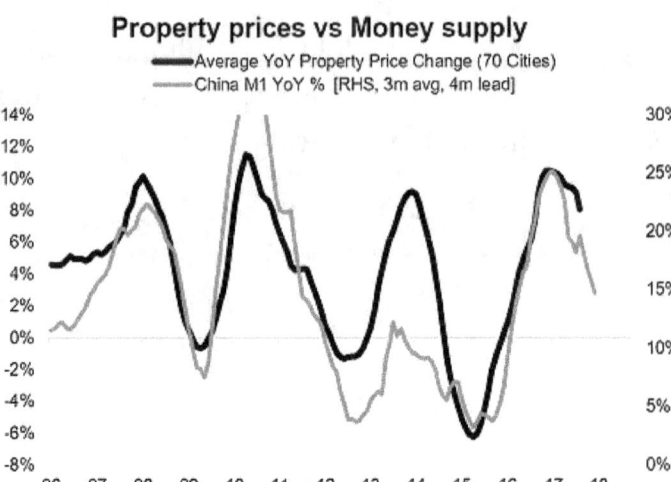

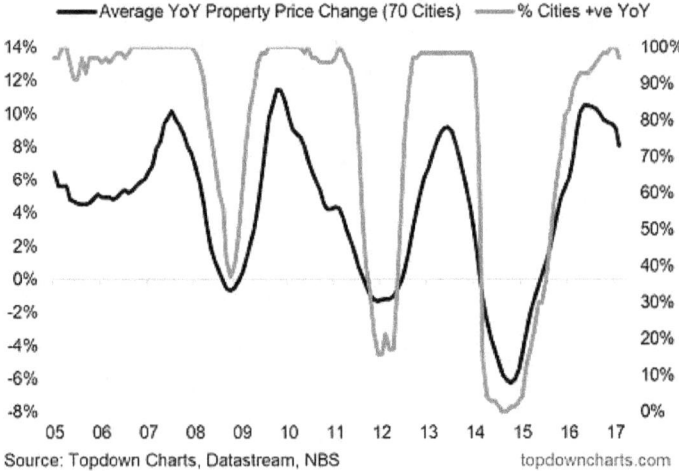

UPSIDE DOWN

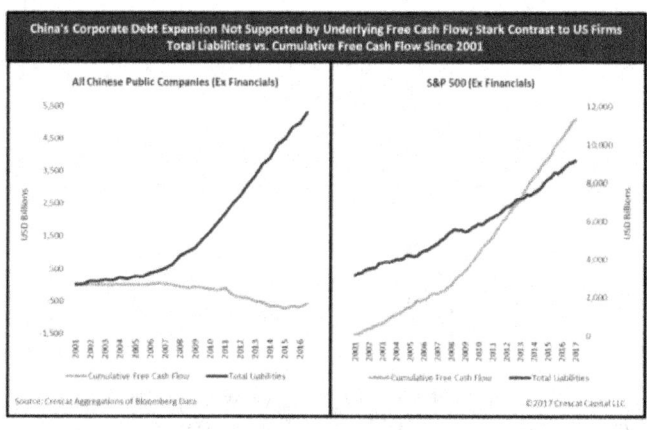

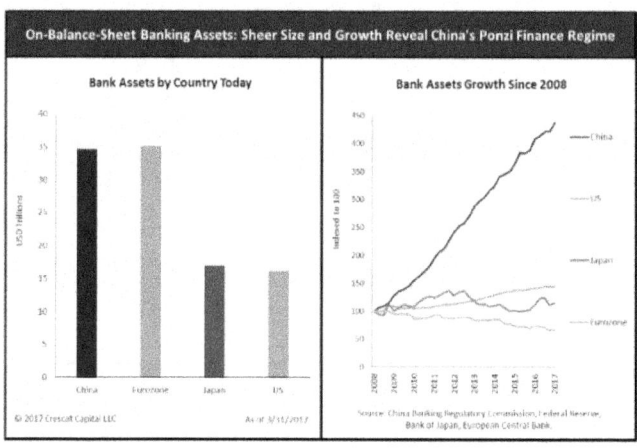

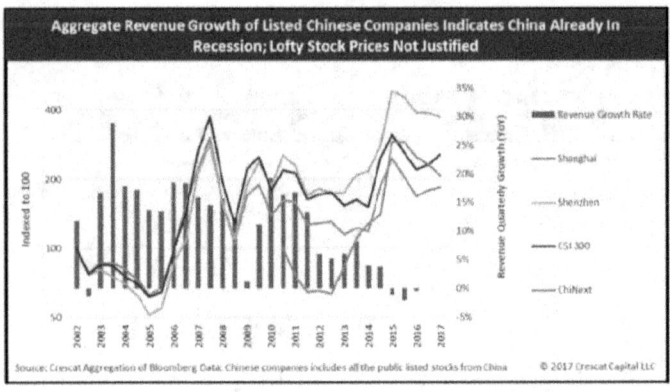

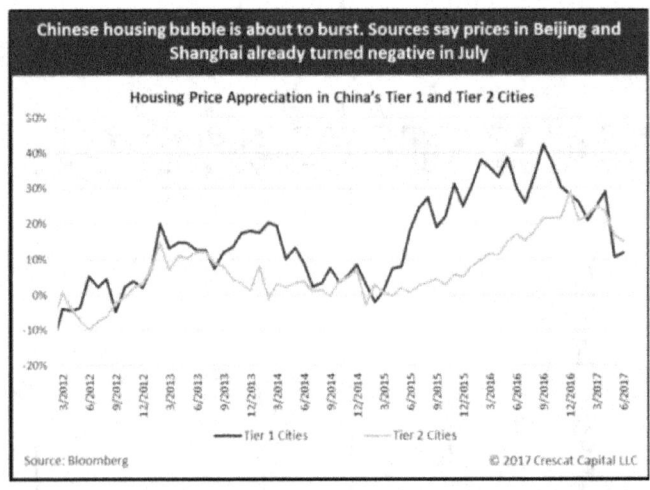

A junk-bond plunge can lead a stock market crash by several months. The high-yield debt market is an important indicator and is looking very unstable, and stocks could drop 10 percent a day. Start to roll out of stocks on any rally!

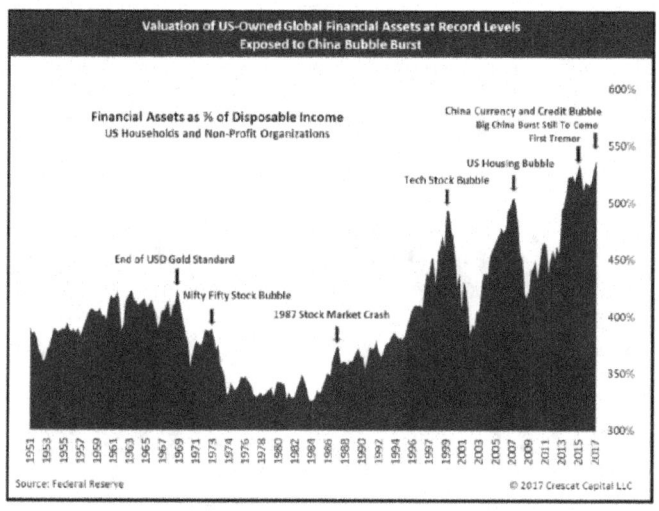

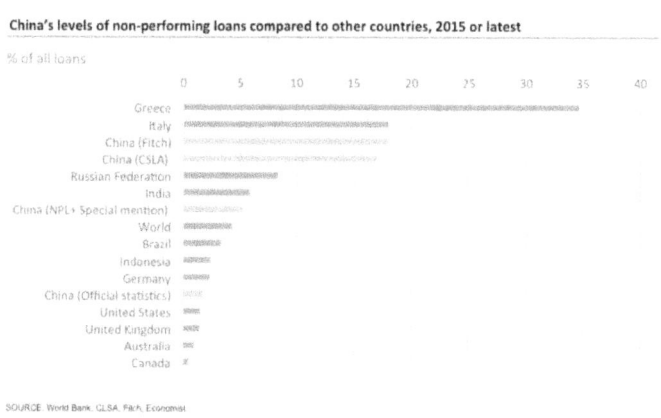

Hedge Funds and the Single-Family Home

Hedge funds have been monopolizing the single-family home market by buying homes in huge numbers, pushing up prices, and taking over two hundred thousand lower priced homes off the market for individual home buyers for a cost of approximately $30 billion.[24]

Initially spending $7.5 billion for forty thousand homes, Blackstone, the biggest hedge fund, pushed prices up a quick 20 percent while individual-home ownership was *dropping*.[25] They then rented these homes back to us, creating a new and dangerous form of securitization—first-rated bonds backed by rental payments. These funds outbid families that had to secure financing, leaving 1 percent of the American institutions earning 95 percent of the property appreciation. According to CoreLogic, the median price in Southern California was $500,000 in June, up 67 percent from 2012—the year the private-equity giant, Blackstone Group, launched Invitation Homes. 26

When this blows up—and it will—thousands of families will be evicted, and these hedge funds are known to be vicious landlords, filing eviction notices to 10 percent of their tenants.

Invitation Homes, also known as Blackstone, was the second-largest portfolio of rental homes with 47,572 homes.[24] And after the merger with Starwood, it owns 82,000 homes valued at $11 billion.27

Homes 4 Rent became the largest fund when they merged with American Residential Properties, Inc. This company is publicly traded and has an inventory of 48,982 homes.[25] The top eighteen institutional funds today own approximately two hundred thousand homes together, and the four largest hedge funds own 145,000, or approximately 75 percent.[26]

After a five-year spending spree, three funds have now invested approximately $1 billion into the Charlotte market alone. These companies paid cash for seven thousand homes across Charlotte with the intent to turn them into rentals with an average rent of $1,400 per month and are now generating about $114 million in return per year while driving up home prices, which will certainly collapse when they exit.[27]

"Every step increases the commodification of these transactions in a way that potentially pits investors with the ability to operate and manage sophisticated trading strategies against everyday homebuyers and homeowners," said Barry Zigas, director of housing for the Consumer Federation of America, about these new investment strategies. [28]

Here's how it might work.

A family rents a single-family home from a hedge fund and then uses down payment assistance from a private-equity firm to buy their first home from an iBuyer*. When the private-equity firm asks for their money back, the family sells their home to an iBuyer and buys a new one owned by the same iBuyer. At each turn, investors extract fees.

Welcome to the Wall Street housing market.

A combination of technology and low interest rates is fueling a surge in this activity. Desperate for higher yields, investors are using computing and data analytics to squeeze returns out of the nest eggs of the middle class.

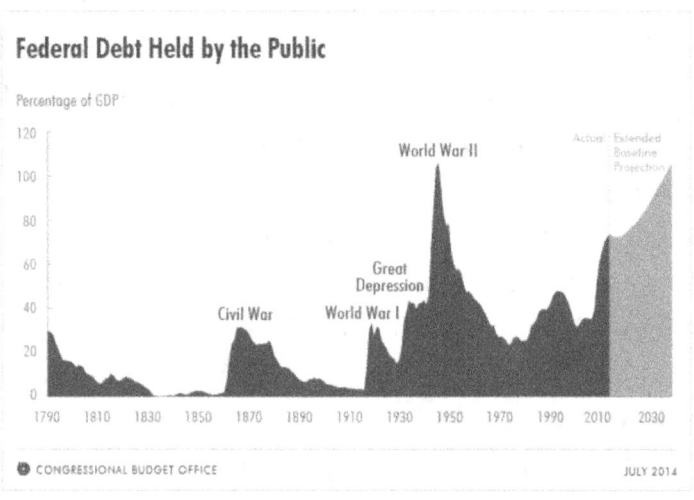

---

* iBuyers are investors that use automated valuation models (AVMs) and other technology to make quick offers on homes, close in days and then resell them.

UPSIDE DOWN

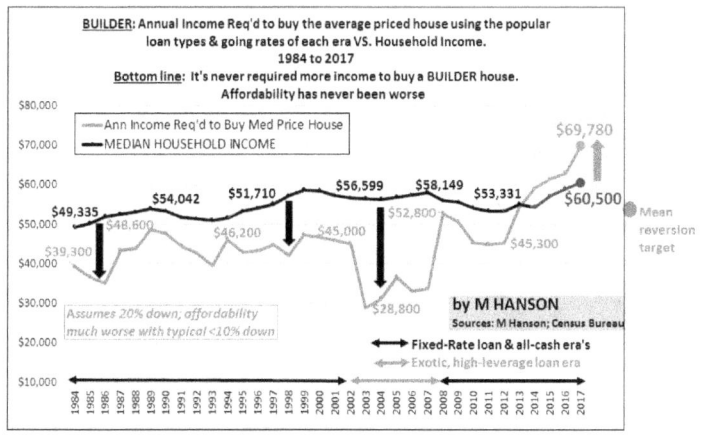

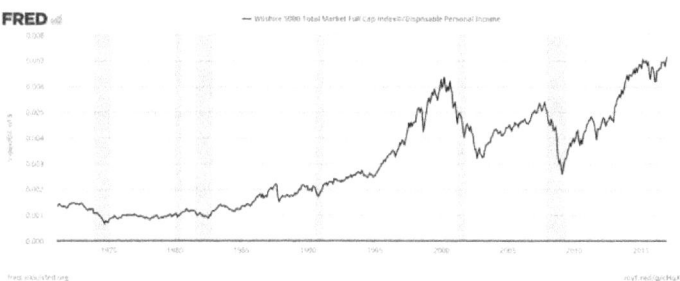

Investing in single-family homes by institutions should be out of bounds and illegal. It destroys the only real investment available to us small fry. First-time homeowners cannot compete with foreign money or hedge funds. Single-family homes must be sacrosanct, and these folks have taken the low hanging fruit right out of your hands!

Conclusion

Real-estate agents attempt to be a calming force since they get paid no matter what conditions are, like the croupier of a gambling establishment. They say, "real-estate prices are only going higher."

Unfortunately, it's the agents themselves who generally buy up homes that are undervalued or require a cash buyer before the potential homeowner even has a chance to see it.

US consumer debt is at $1 trillion, an all-time high. Plus, debt to disposable income is at a record 188.7 percent.[29]

The best equation for real home values is ten times annual rent. For example, consider when rent is $2,000 per month. Annual rent would be $24,000. Then $240,000 would be the median home value.

Median household income has been falling as real-estate values rise. What an ominous sign—during this massive property boom, our household income has been stagnant.[30] The median home price in Sydney, Australia, is now above $1 million![31]

Remember, the Fed has kept interest rates at zero percent for seven years, fueling this extraordinary rally in assets. Investors have bought up supply and tightened the market. Forget about comps that appraisers use to determine home values—it's all a house of cards.

In my opinion, the housing crash will begin in earnest by the end of 2018. Put your home on the market now, and enjoy multiple offers over the asking price. Sell before everyone catches on. Buyers, don't get caught up in this frenzy. If you wait a few years to buy, you will be justly rewarded.

NOTES

1. http://www.thetruthaboutmortgage.com/dti-debt-to-income-ratio/

2. http://www.mercurynews.com/2017/09/14/tip-of-the-iceberg-more-on-the-sunnyvale-house-that-sold-for-782000-over-asking-and-what-it-all-means/February 24, 2017

3. www.zerohedge.com/.../starwood-reit-ceo-high-end-manhattan-condo-market-catastr. Feb 24, 2017

4. Thomas Gibson, *The Facts About Speculation*, 1923.Cosimo Classics

5. https://www.bloomberg.com/.../-deep-sub-prime-car-loans-hit-crisis-era-milestone-as-... August 15 2017

6. www.businessinsider.com/subprime-auto-loans-are-a-reminder-of-the-housing-crisis-... Apr 15, 2017

7. https://realinvestmentadvice.com/markets-overlooking-a-clear-present-danger/Mar 30, 2017

8. Citigroup Has More Derivatives than 4,701 U.S. Banks Combined ... wallstreetonparade.com/.../citigroup-has-more-derivatives-than-4701-u-s-banks-comb...
Jul 14, 2016

9. https://www.cnbc.com/.../robert-shiller-with-stock-valuations-high-its-time-to- reduce-..Feb 24, 2017

10. https://dailyreckoning.com/charts-prove-financial-bubbles Jan 31, 2017

11. https://www.cnbc.com/.../goldman-sachs-calls-warren-buffetts-favorite-method-to-val...
Jun 28, 2017

12. https://www.cnbc.com/.../any-way-you-look-at-it-this-stock-market-is-overvalued-gol...Jul 24, 2017

13. https://www.cnbc.com/.../any-way-you-look-at-it-this-stock-market-is-overvalued-gol...Jul 24, 2017

14. www.marketwatch.com › Investing › Stocks › Brett Arends's ROI Mar 14, 2017

15. secure.marketwatch.com/.../this-is-the-most-overvalued-stock-market-on-record-even-w... Mar 14, 2017

16. www.marketwatch.com › Markets › U.S. & Canada › Market Extra Jul 20, 2017

17. http://secure.marketwatch.com/story/the-us-stock-market-is-the-worlds-most-expensive-2017-07-18?link=emailMidSection

18. https://www.cnbc.com/id/104402550?view=story&$DEVICE$=native-android...Apr 13, 2017.

19. https://www.cnbc.com/.../chinas-debt-surpasses-300-percent-of-gdp-iif-says-raising-d... Jun 28, 2017

20. https://dailyreckoning.com/charts-prove-financial-bubbles/
Jan 31, 2017

21. https://www.federalreserve.gov/monetarypolicy/fomcminutes20161214.htm Jan 4, 2017

22. thehill.com/.../pundits.../economy.../332505-china-is-far-away-but-its-bursting-bubbl...May 9, 2017

23. https://financialtribune.com/.../china-needs-rapid-growth-to-ease-huge-debt-bubble Sep 3, 2017

24. https://www.inman.com/2017/06/09/welcome-to-wall-streets-housing-market/Jun 9, 2017

25. https://boingboing.net/2017/09/18/invitation-homes.html

26. www.sandiegouniontribune.com/.../real.../sd-fi-median-december-20170123-story.ht..Jan 24, 2017

27. https://www.forbes.com/.../single-family-rental-leaders-invitation-homes-starwood-wa... Aug 10, 2017

28. https://www.inman.com/2017/06/09/welcome-to-wall-streets-housing-market/Jun 9, 2017

29. financialpost.com › Debt › Personal Finance Mar 15, 2017

30. lemoore-realestate.com/real-estate.../real-estate/rising-rents-stagnant-wages-and-the-bu... Sep 27, 2017

31. www.news.com.au/.../sydney...house-prices.../b647a530d1fedc744540742d89eef0a5 Jun 26, 2017

a. July 22, 2017, https:https://www.benzinga.com/analyst-ratings/analyst-color/17/07/9784480/different-market-same-story-subprime-auto-loan-defaults-

b. April 15, 2017, www.businessinsider.com/subprime-auto-loans-are-a-reminder-of-the-housing-crisis-....

c. https://realinvestmentadvice.com/markets-overlooking-a-clear-present-danger/ Mar 30 2017

8. July 14, 2016, wallstreetonparade.com/.../citigroup-has-mor

9. February 24, 2017, https://www.cnbc.com/.../robert-shiller-with-stock-valuations-high-its-time-to-reduce-...

10. July 24, 2017, https://www.cnbc.com/.../anyway-you-look-at-it-this-stock-market-is-overvalued-gol...

11. See note 11.

12. See note 11

13. https://www.hussmanfunds.com/wmc/wmc170313.htm.www.marketwatch.com › Investing › Stocks › Brett Arends's ROI Mar 14 2017 www.starcapital.de/research/stockmarketvaluation Jul 20, 2017

15. https://www.cnbc.com/id/104402550?view=story&$DEVICE$=native-android...

16. June 28, 2017, https://www.cnbc.com/.../chinas-debt-surpasses-300-percent-of-gdp-iif-says-raising-d...

17. October 19, 2016, www.telegraph.co.uk/.../fed-risks-repeating-lehman-blunder-as-us-recession-storm-ga...

18. July 7, 2017, https://www.federalreserve.gov/monetarypolicy/2017-07-mpr-part1.htm.

19. November 29, 2013, www.motherjones.com/politics/2013/11/wall-street-buying-foreclosed-homes/.

20. August 10, 2017, https://www.forbes.com/.../single-family-rental-leaders-invitation-homes-starwood-wa...

21. February 1, 2017, https://www.biggerpockets.com/.../54589-invitation-homes-blackstone-s-acquisition-o...

22. See note 23.

23. February 1, 2017, https://www.biggerpockets.com/.../54589-invitation-homes-blackstone-s-acquisition-o..27, 2017, lemoore-realestate.com/.../rising-rents-stagnant-wages-and-the-burden-of-unstable-ho...June 26, 2017

29. financialpost.com › Debt › Personal Finance Mar 15, 2017

30. www.sbs.com.au/yourlanguage/korean/en/.../median-price-sydney-home-above-1m Jun 29, 2017

www.ingramcontent.com/pod-product-compliance
Lightning Source LLC
Chambersburg PA
CBHW050022230526
45470CB00003B/1082